ADVENTURES IN NATURE

EXPLORING PONDS

BY JEN GREEN AND LIA VISIRIN

WINDMILL BOOKS

Published in 2026 by Windmill Books,
an Imprint of Rosen Publishing
2544 Clinton St.
Buffalo, NY 14224

First published in Great Britain in 2025 by Hodder & Stoughton

Credits
Series Editor: Grace Kelly
Series Designer: Peter Scoulding

Cataloging-in-Publication Data
Names: Green, Jen, author. | Visirin, Lia, illustrator.
Title: Exploring ponds / Jen Green, illustrated by Lia Visirin.
Description: Buffalo, NY : Windmill Books, 2026. | Series: Adventures in nature | Includes glossary and index.
Identifiers: ISBN 9781538398746 (pbk.) | ISBN 9781538398753 (library bound) | ISBN 9781538398760 (ebook)
Subjects: LCSH: Pond ecology--Juvenile literature. | Pond animals--Juvenile literature. | Nature study--Juvenile literature.
Classification: LCC QH541.5.P63 G743 2026 | DDC 577.63'6--dc23

Printed in the United States of America

CPSIA Compliance Information: Batch #CSWM26
For Further Information contact Rosen Publishing at 1-800-237-9932

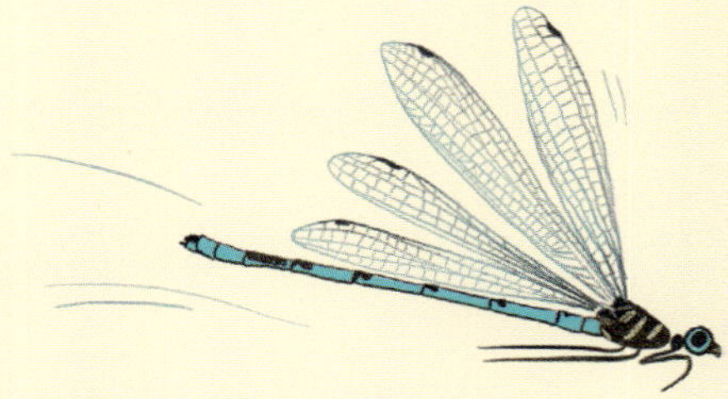

CONTENTS

AT THE POND

A pond is a hole or hollow filled with fresh water. Some ponds are made by people. Others form naturally when rainwater fills a hollow. Ponds are full of plants and animals, so they are a perfect place to study wildlife!

Trees such as willows and alders grow by ponds. They need a lot of water and don't mind their roots getting wet!

Ponds contain still or very slow-moving water. Most are quite shallow with a muddy bottom.

All animals, including these baby swans, or cygnets, need food, water, and shelter. Ponds provide all three, so it's no wonder many creatures live here!

This symbol shows when extra care is needed. Always be careful near water and never go without a parent or caregiver. Take good care of nature too — don't pick plants, and never handle wild creatures.

When looking for nature at the pond, you will need waterproof clothing, sneakers or waterproof boots, a hat, sunglasses, and sunscreen. Make notes and drawings using a notebook, pen, and colored pencils. A magnifying glass, phone camera, fishing net, and a collecting jar will also come in handy.

ON THE BANK

Ponds contain several minihabitats, such as banks, surface waters, and the bottom. Each has its own plants and animals. Grass, reeds, and flowering plants grow by ponds. Some animals spend their lives on the bank. Others just visit to drink.

Water voles live in burrows by the water's edge. These little mammals are quite rare.

These mammals visit ponds to drink, and leave their prints in the mud (see page 7). You may also see the tracks of voles, water shrews, and birds.

A FOX'S PRINTS ARE SIMILAR TO THOSE OF A DOG.

A DEER LEAVES DEEP, NARROW HOOF PRINTS.

AN OTTER HAS LARGE PAWS WITH FIVE CLAWED TOES.

Mud can be very slippery. Be careful by the water's edge.

Ponds vary in size from millponds to tiny garden pools like this one.

Dragonflies patrol along the bank of a pond, catching insects.

WHAT DO YOU SEE?

Footprints can be used to identify wildlife long after the animals have gone. Compare the prints you find with the ones shown here. Find more prints in wildlife books or on the internet.

FLOATING AT THE SURFACE

Plants, such as weeds and water lilies, float on the pond's surface. Some insects are so light that they can skim across the surface without sinking. Frogs rest on lily pads and wait for passing insects to eat.

A lily leaf is called a pad.

Lily leaves and flowers float on water. The long stems reach down to roots buried in the mud.

DO YOU THINK THE WATER PLANTS ARE FLOATING FREELY OR FIXED TO THE BED OF THE POND?

A water strider, or pond skater, is an insect with long legs and a lightweight body. It slides across the water surface, which acts like a thin skin.

WHAT DO YOU SEE?

Use a magnifying glass to study small creatures at the surface. Make notes and sketches of what you see. Loud noises and sudden movements will frighten animals. The quieter you are, the more you will see!

When an insect comes within range, a frog shoots out its long, sticky tongue.

Frogs have long legs for swimming and leaping.

BELOW THE SURFACE

Many kinds of minibeast live just below the water's surface. Like all animals, they need to breathe oxygen. Some take air from the surface. Some carry a bubble of air down with them. Others take oxygen from the water using gills, as fish do.

The water scorpion breathes air at the surface using the long, thin tube on its tail.

The tube acts like a snorkel.

These minibeasts live near the surface.

A DIVING BEETLE STORES AIR UNDER ITS WINGS.

A WATER SCORPION BREATHES AIR USING THE LONG TUBES ON ITS TAIL.

A WATER SPIDER SPINS A TINY NET WHICH IT FILLS WITH AIR.

HOW MANY INSECTS CAN YOU NAME THAT LIVE IN PONDS?

Take care around pond creatures. They are delicate and some can bite.

Pond snails swim about using their soft, rubbery foot. They use their long feelers for sensing.

Mayflies are insects whose young grow up in water. Young mayflies, called larvae, breathe using three feathery gills on their tail.

WHAT DO YOU SEE?

Fill your collecting jar with pond water. Sweep your net gently across the surface. Empty it into the jar. Study the creatures you have caught with a magnifying glass. Then return them safely to the pond.

ON STONES AND PLANTS

Ponds contain all sorts of minibeasts. Shrimps and worms lurk under stones or in the mud. Snails crawl over plants. Some of these small creatures are plant-eaters. Others are meat-eating predators.

Pond snails feed on tiny plants that they scrape off rocks. They creep along on their muscular foot.

Garden snails also like wet places and visit ponds to feed on plants.

A hard shell protects the snail's soft body.

Crane flies have long, thin legs and bodies. They are also known as daddy longlegs.

These creepers and crawlers live on pond plants and stones.

A LEECH SWIMS BY WRIGGLING ITS BODY.

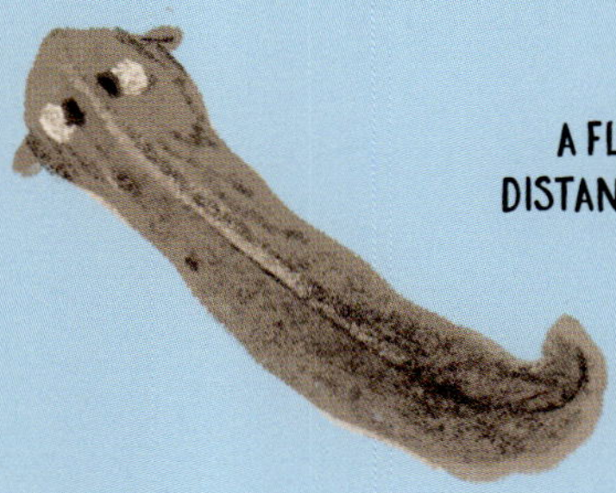

A FLATWORM IS A DISTANT COUSIN OF THE LEECH.

A WATER SHRIMP HAS MANY LEGS AND A SEE-THROUGH BODY.

A YOUNG CADDISFLY LIVES IN A SILK CASE. IT STICKS STONES AND TWIGS TO THE OUTSIDE AS A DISGUISE.

WHAT DO YOU SEE?

Fill your collecting jar with pond water, then sweep your net along the bottom of a pond. Empty the contents into your jar. You can also lift up stones to find some lurking creatures. Group the minibeasts you find under these headings:

- Insects
- Worms
- Shrimps
- Snails

IN DEEP WATER

Fish, frogs, and newts lurk in deep water. These skilled swimmers dive down to find food or hide from enemies. Frogs, toads, and newts all belong to a group of animals called amphibians.

Adult newts live mainly on land, but lay their eggs in the pond. Their young grow up in the water.

These strong swimmers hunt for food in the pond.

NEWTS FEED ON TADPOLES, SMALL FISH, AND WORMS.

THIS FROG HAS MOIST SKIN.
TOADS HAVE DRY, WARTY SKIN.

A STICKLEBACK HAS SILVERY SPINES ON ITS BACK.

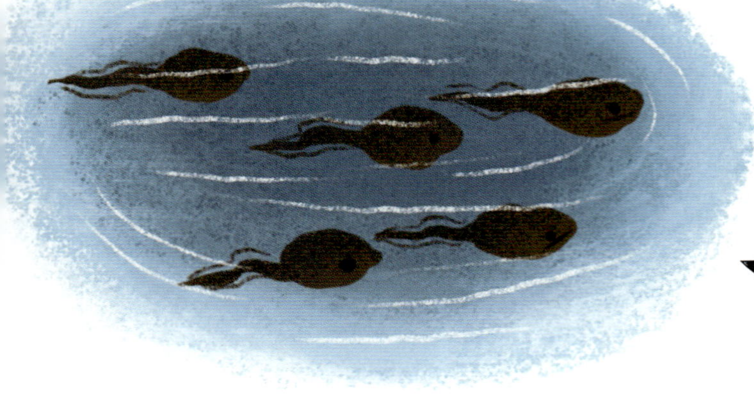

Young frogs or toads are called tadpoles. They have a long tail that helps them to swim through the water.

Water shrews dive underwater to hunt fish, tadpoles, snails, and insects. These little mammals are always hungry!

WHAT DO YOU SEE?

Water shrews and voles live in burrows on the bank. Birds, such as kingfishers, live on the bank, too. If you are quiet and patient you may be able to spot the burrow-owner. Binoculars will help!

HOW CAN YOU TELL FROGS FROM TOADS?

IN AND OUT OF THE WATER

Dragonflies are the pond's most spectacular insects. Their cousins, damselflies, are smaller but just as beautiful. Like frogs and newts, these insects grow up in water, and then live on land as adults.

WHAT DO YOU SEE?

Adult dragonflies live by water and hunt flying insects. They are large and quite bold, so they are easy to spot. You can also look for cast-off dragonfly skins among water plants.

Dragonflies grow up to 4 inches (10 cm) across. They can fly at 19 miles (30 km) per hour! Damselflies are smaller and more delicate. Both catch flying insects, which they crunch up in their toothed jaws.

Huge eyes cover most of the head.

Large, see-through wings.

In spring and summer dragonflies mate at the water's surface. The female dragonfly lays its eggs by dipping its tail in the water.

DRAGONFLIES CAN BE RED, GREEN, BLUE, OR YELLOW. WHAT COLOR ARE THE ONES YOU SEE?

The young damselfly, called a nymph, grows up in the pond. When fully grown, it crawls up a stem. Its skin splits to reveal the adult insect, which spreads its wings and flies away.

DABBLING AT THE SURFACE

When people think of ponds, they often think of ducks! Some ducks feed by sucking in food at the surface, called dabbling. Others dive down to the bottom. Both divers and dabblers are perfectly suited to swimming in ponds.

Mallards are the most common ducks. The female (right) has brown feathers. The male (below) is brightly colored so he is easy to spot.

CAN YOU DESCRIBE THE DIFFERENCE BETWEEN THE FEMALE AND THE MALE MALLARD DUCKS?

WHAT DO YOU SEE?

Take some seeds, oats, peas, or rice to the pond to feed to the ducks. Watch how they eat. Some ducks will dive down for food. How long do they stay underwater?

Some ducks upend to feed just below the surface. Their waterproof feathers help to keep them dry.

Ducklings take to water soon after they hatch.

AMONG THE REEDS

Reeds and bulrushes grow by the water. These tall plants make it hard to see pond birds, frogs, and other animals, but the animals' calls may give them away.

Reeds and bulrushes grow up to 10 feet (3 m) tall. They form a dense screen by the water.

A bulrush's brown spike holds the seeds.

CAN YOU IDENTIFY ANY SOUNDS YOU HEAR AMONG THE REEDS?

The female mallard's brown, speckled feathers help to hide her while she is sitting on her nest.

WHAT DO YOU HEAR?

Birds, frogs, and other animals can be identified by their calls. Frogs croak to attract a mate in spring. Ducks quack, while bitterns make an amazing booming sound. The coot's loud call sounds like its name.

Moorhens and coots live among the reeds. These birds can be easy to confuse, but the coot has a white patch above its bill. A moorhen has a red beak and yellow legs.

AT THE LAKE

Lakes are large areas of fresh water. They are usually deeper than ponds and contain slow-moving water. Lakes have many amazing creatures. Long-necked birds feed by the water. Large fish, such as carp and pike, lurk in the depths.

Geese and swans have webbed feet. They are strong swimmers, but walk with a waddle on land.

These large, long-necked birds live by lakes.

A HERON WADES IN THE SHALLOWS AND SPEARS FISH WITH ITS LONG BEAK.

A MUTE SWAN FEEDS ON WATER PLANTS

A CANADA GOOSE EATS WATERWEED, GRASS, AND SEEDS.

HERONS, GEESE, AND SWANS ALL HAVE LONG NECKS. HOW COULD THIS HELP WITH FEEDING?

Young geese (above) and swans have fluffy, gray-brown feathers.

WHAT DO YOU SEE?

Use your binoculars to study water birds. Make notes and sketches. Listen out for calls, such as honks and hisses. Wearing sunglasses will cut down reflections and help you to spot fish.

Adult mute swans have pure white feathers.

Lakes and ponds can both contain deep water. Be very careful near the edge.

LIFE CYCLES

The best time to study pond life is in spring and summer, when animals have their young. Frogs, newts, and insects pass through several stages in their life cycle. Birds, such as swans, take great care of their young.

Young swans, called cygnets, hatch after about a month. They are able to fly four months later but don't get their white feathers until the following year.

Pond birds lay their eggs in the spring.

Swans defend their nest and young fiercely, so don't get too close.

WHAT DO YOU SEE?

Can you find some frogspawn in a nearby pond or river? Watch as the tadpoles grow up.

Frogs lay masses of jelly-coated eggs in water. The eggs hatch into tadpoles. After about five weeks, the legs start to appear. The tail shrinks and the animal becomes a tiny frog.

WHAT ANIMALS CAN YOU THINK OF THAT GROW UP IN WATER AND THEN LIVE ON LAND?

Mayflies lay their eggs in water. The young (see page 11) spend up to three years growing up in the pond. As adults they live for just one or two days!

FOOD CHAINS

Living things in a pond form a web of life. As in other wild places, the rule is eat or be eaten! Plants provide food for herbivores (plant-eaters), such as worms, caterpillars, and many insects. These in turn may be eaten by carnivores (meat-eaters), such as herons and pike.

This gray heron has caught a frog. Frogs, in turn, hunt insects, such as flies.

Caterpillars (young insects) eat leaves.

TRY THIS

Draw a simple food chain showing a heron, frog, and fly. Now try drawing food chains of other pond creatures (you need to know what each animal eats).

Food chains show the links between living things. This pond food chain shows a kingfisher, stickleback, and mosquitoes. The red arrows show who eats what.

NATURE DIARY

Ponds are busiest in spring and summer, as plants grow and animals are born. Build up a picture of pond life throughout the year by keeping a diary.

KEEP NOTES

Always take your notebook with you. Record the date, time, weather, and place. Describe what you see.

This plant is called a flag iris. It produces yellow flowers in early summer and is found near ponds.

Make a collection of finds, such as feathers and pond leaves, to stick in your diary.

TOP TIPS

- Hide behind reeds, trees, or bushes to get close to animals without being spotted.
- Listen for the calls of birds, frogs, and other animals.
- Don't forget to look for tracks in the mud.

In winter, ponds and lakes may freeze over, and animals, such as frogs are asleep.

MAKE A MINI POND

If you can, make a mini pond in your school garden or at home using an old washing-up bowl filled with water. Put gravel and some bigger stones at the bottom and add some water plants. Water animals will soon move in!

GLOSSARY

Algae tiny plant-like organisms that live in water.

Amphibian one of a group of animals that live on land, but lay their eggs in the water. Frogs, toads, and newts are all amphibians.

Bill another name for a beak.

Burrow a hole or tunnel in the ground where a small animal might live.

Carnivore an animal that eats meat.

Dabbling when a duck feeds at the surface by sucking water through its bill.

Gills the feathery structures that fish and some insects use to breathe underwater.

Habitat the natural home of a plant or animal, such as a pond or a wood.

Herbivore an animal that eats plants.

Larva (plural larvae) a young animal, such as an insect.

Mammal an animal with hair on its body. Baby mammals drink their mother's milk.

Millpond a large pool of calm water.

Oxygen a gas found in the air and also mixed in water. All animals need to breathe oxygen.

Predator an animal that hunts other animals for food.

Webbed feet when an animal has skin between its toes, so its feet work like paddles.

FIND OUT MORE

Books

Explore Ecosystems: In a Pond by Sarah Ridley, Wayland, 2023

The Great Outdoors: Lakes and Ponds by Lisa Regan, Wayland, 2020

Pond Life to Spot by Kate Nolan and Steph Fizer Coleman, Usborne, 2021

Websites

kids.nationalgeographic.com/nature/habitats/article/freshwater
A look at freshwater habitats and their wildlife.

https://www.rspb.org.uk/helping-nature/what-you-can-do/activities/pond-dipping
Discover pond life with this fun, pond-dipping guide from the Royal Society for the Protection of Birds.

kids.britannica.com/kids/article/pond-life/476304
Learn more about life in a pond.

NOTE: Every effort has been made by the Publishers to ensure that the websites on page 31 of this book are suitable for children, that they are of the highest educational value, and that they contain no inappropriate or offensive material. However, because of the nature of the Internet, it is impossible to guarantee that the contents of these sites will not be altered. We strongly advise that Internet access is supervised by a responsible adult.

INDEX